IRELAND IN THE EUROPEAN COMMUNITY

Performance, prospects and strategy

SUMMARY OF MAIN POINTS

TABLE OF CONTENTS

PREFACE

PART I: BACKGROUND

TABLE OF CONTENTS

PART IV: POLICY RESPONSES

PUBLISHED BY THE NATIONAL ECONOMIC AND SOCIAL COUNCIL

Copies of this Report may be obtained from
THE NATIONAL ECONOMIC AND SOCIAL COUNCIL
Earl Court, Adelaide Road, Dublin 2.
or The Government Publications Sales Office.
Price: £5.00

Preface

The National Economic and Social Council is made up of the main interest groups in society: trade unions, employers, agricultural representatives and Government nominees, including one from the National Youth Council of Ireland. It was established in 1973 to provide a forum in which the efficient development of the national economy and the achievement of social justice could be discussed and the Government advised on these matters. This advisory function is performed through the presentation of reports to the Government and through direct discussion with the Taoiseach and cabinet ministers. Since its inception, the Council has produced over eighty reports on a wide variety of issues, including general economic and social policy, industrial policy, policies on natural resources and various sectoral issues.

In May 1987, the Taoiseach requested the NESC to undertake a project on Ireland and the European Community. The terms of reference for the project were:

(i) to undertake an in-depth study of Ireland's comparative performance in the EC, incorporating an assessment of the impact on Ireland of membership of the Community;

(ii) to assess the problems and opportunities inherent in unification of the internal market;

(iii) to put forward and evaluate the policy options available to help mitigate the problems, capitalise on the opportunities and consider what countervailing measures may be necessary.

The Report was published in September 1989. Herewith is published a Summary of the major points and arguments. The Summary is divided into four parts. Part I provides background information on the current phase of European integration. Part II examines the effects of membership of the European Community on Ireland's economic structure and performance. Such an exercise is a necessary prelude to assessing the threats and opportunities which will emerge with completion of the internal market by 1992, and to our consideration of the policy issues which arise at the national and Community level. Chapter 2 discusses the possible effects of economic integration. Chapter 3 sets out the basic facts of Ireland's performance since 1973 and Ireland's performance in the Community relative to that of other countries.

Chapter 4 sets out the Council's conclusions on the impact of EC membership, concentrating on those activities most influenced by integration into the Community i.e. manufacturing, agriculture and trade. The lessons to be learned from the overall analysis of the 1973-87 period are presented in Chapter 5.

Part III of the report examines the threats and opportunities likely to arise from the completion of the European internal market by 1992. In order to identify these, we begin, in Chapter 6, with presentation and explanation of a framework for analysis of the effects of market completion on the Irish economy. This analytical framework is based on identification of the direct and indirect effects of the removal of the remaining barriers to trade. We believe that Chapter 6 provides a framework which can be used by those who wish to study the implications of 1992 for the particular sectors with which they are concerned.

While the report is *not* intended to be a detailed study of the *sectoral* implications of market completion, we do apply our analytical framework to selected sectors. In Chapter 7 we consider which parts of manufacturing industry face threats and which parts face opportunities - and whether these arise from the completion of the internal market or from other sources.

In Chapter 8 we examine the services sector. It is widely agreed that 1992 will be more significant in services than in manufacturing - given the present highly segmented European market for most services. Our analysis confirms that distribution, transport and financial services will all experience profound changes in the coming years.

Chapter 9 asks the important question: how will market completion affect the regions of Europe? We explain and evaluate arguments concerning regional convergence and divergence and consider some of the empirical evidence on this question. Our conclusion is that the costs and benefits of the completion of the market are likely to be distributed unevenly - and, consequently, it should not be expected to narrow the disparities between regions, let alone bring about convergence. This is a fundamental conclusion which informs the rest of the report.

Part III of the report concludes with Chapter 10, which studies the issue of the removal of frontiers - and the approximation of indirect tax which is considered necessary to achieve it. Both the need for the removal of frontiers and the effects of indirect tax approximation on Ireland are evaluated.

Part IV of the Summary considers the major policy issues which arise from the analysis undertaken in Parts II and III. Chapter 11 outlines the overall or strategic approach to European economic integration which, in the Council's view, Ireland should adopt. The Council's advocacy of advanced economic and monetary union informs its approach to other policy issues and, consequently, Chapter 11 is the core of the report.

In Chapter 12 we consider the appropriate corporate and public policy responses to the specific threats and opportunities identified in Part III. This chapter focusses on manufacturing, services and agriculture. The appropriate policy approach to EC tax approximation is set out in Chapter 10. In Chapter 13 we consider both national and Community policies to achieve economic cohesion and convergence. While this involves a review of EC structural and regional policy, it also includes an assessment of the significance of other policy approaches. From the material a number of policy issues arising for Ireland and the Community are identified and discussed.

Chapter 14 considers the social dimension of the Community's internal market programme. The content and meaning of the social dimension is explained and some important policy issues are identified. Drawing on the strategic approach to integration set out in Chapter 11, we outline how the social dimension of the EC should be viewed by Ireland. Some concluding remarks are presented in Chapter 15.

The Summary has also one other objective: to correct some erroneous interpretations of the report by some commentators. These arise, in particular, in regard to the impact of Community Membership on Ireland (see pages 27 and 28) and to the rationale for the strategic approach advocated by the Council. (see page 59).

PART I

Background

The Current Phase of European Integration

THE DEVELOPMENT OF THE COMMUNITY

1. Background

The Treaty of Rome, signed by Belgium, France, Germany, Italy, Luxembourg and the Netherlands in 1957, expressed the determination to "lay the foundations of an ever closer union among the peoples of Europe". The means chosen to pursue this aim was the establishment of a European Economic Community. The central element was to be the creation of a common market - an integrated market without obstacles to the movement of goods, persons, services and capital. Another important feature of the Treaty was agreement to adopt a common policy for agriculture and transport, and to devise a system to ensure that competition in the common market was not distorted. In the beginning, progress towards establishment of the common market was rapid - tariffs and quotas being abolished ahead of schedule. This coincided with a period of strong economic growth in Europe.

In the early 1970s the economic climate deteriorated sharply after the break-up of the international system of monetary management and the first oil crisis. The Community was enlarged in 1973 to include Ireland, Britain and Denmark. In the late 1970s and early 1980s, further severe inflation and recession were experienced. Progress towards European economic integration came to a halt. Obstacles to trade in services and capital and to the free movement of persons were not removed. Indeed, even free movement of goods and undistorted competition in industrial production were eroded by governments' resort to state aids of various kinds in the face of severe industrial and employment crises. Not only was agreement not forthcoming on further progress to economic integration, but the Community became embroiled in continual and deep disputes on budgetary contributions and agricultural prices.

During the early 1980s it became widely accepted that one of the main obstacles to the economic growth of European countries was 'non-Europe'. By 'non-Europe' was meant the low level of co-operation between Community members and the weakness of common policies. The members of the Community had responded to the slow growth and high inflation of the 1970s by *reducing* rather than increasing their co-operation.

In devising a strategy for recovery, stress was laid on the creation of a unified internal market and new Community co-operation in a number of fields. In addition, there was strong pressure for reform of the EC's institutions.

2. Completing the Internal Market

In 1985 the incoming Commission adopted a Programme with the completion of the internal market as its centre-piece and presented a comprehensive White Paper to the European Council entitled *Completing the Internal Market*. The major contribution of the White Paper was to set out in great detail the measures necessary to achieve completion of the internal market and to adopt a timetable for the legal enactment of these measures such that the internal market would be completed by 1992.

While the Commission's White Paper was concerned mainly with the completion of the internal market, it also linked this to three other approaches which are of significance in the current phase of European integration. First, it stressed that the abolition of internal borders must be accompanied by actions which strengthen the research and technological base of the Community's industry. Second, it argued that the integration of national markets must be accompanied by a strengthening of the co-ordination of economic policies and the European Monetary System (EMS). Third, the Commission noted the risk that, by facilitating the movement of resources to areas of greatest economic advantage, the completion of the internal market could widen the existing disparities between regions of the Community. In the Commission's view this enhanced the importance of the Community's Structural Funds.

3. The Internal Market White Paper

The White Paper grouped the 300 measures necessary to complete the internal market under three headings:

(a) the removal of physical barriers;
(b) the removal of technical barriers;
(c) the removal of fiscal barriers.

The most obvious example of physical barriers are customs posts at frontiers. It was proposed that customs posts be abolished both to reduce delays at frontiers and to remove the most visible sign of the continued division of the Community. However, customs checks exist because of the different indirect tax regimes and different technical and safety standards in different member states. Consequently, removal of physical barriers (frontier checks) requires the removal of fiscal barriers. It is for this reason that the Commission's internal market programme includes proposals for the approximation of indirect taxes across the Community.

Examples of technical barriers are the different standards for individual products adopted in different member states for health or safety reasons, or for environmental or consumer protection. These clearly protect certain producers and limit competition across frontiers. Another set of technical barriers are the national rules and regulations which restrict the provision of services across national boundaries.

A very significant set of barriers to trade and competition are those which arise because of the nature of government procurement. In principle, public bodies are already forbidden to discriminate between suppliers from Community countries when purchasing many goods or services and are required to advertise major contracts throughout the Community. In practice, public procurement in all EC countries has favoured national companies wherever possible. In addition, very important areas, such as telecommunications, water, energy and transport, were exempt from the Community's requirements for open tendering. The White Paper proposed that existing regulations for open competition would have to be enforced and that these exemptions would be eliminated. These are, potentially, very significant measures because one of the central economic arguments for completion of the internal market is that European firms in advanced products such as telecommunications, energy and transport are (as a result of the fragmentation of the market) too small to compete with major non-European producers.

THE SINGLE EUROPEAN ACT

The three themes which emerged from the discussion of the problems of the Community in the late seventies and early eighties, were the completion of the internal market, institutional reform, and the development of new Community policies in a number of fields. Each was reflected in the revision of the Treaty in the Single European Act.

1. The Internal Market

The Single European Act added new articles to the Treaty of Rome explicitly addressing the programme for an internal market. These new articles are of two types. The first type set December 1992 as the target date for establishing the internal market. The second group of new articles were added to the Treaty in order to make sure that the decisions necessary to complete the internal market are actually taken at the European Council. These provide for a move from unanimity to qualified majority voting on many issues related to the internal market.

However, the Single European Act (SEA) explicitly limited the extension of majority voting by stating that it shall not apply to fiscal and taxation matters, monetary co-operation, the free movement of persons, the rights and interests of employed persons, the environment, the level of finance for research and development, and the co-ordination of the Structural Funds.

2. Institutional Reform

The extension of majority voting was one major element of institutional reform designed to increase the effectiveness of the Community's decision-taking procedures. A second reform provides for a 'co-operation procedure' between the Council of Ministers and the European Parliament.

3. New Treaty Aims and Policies

The SEA provided a stronger treaty basis for Community action in the fields of research, the environment, regional policy and some aspects of social policy.

Economic and Social Cohesion

In the White Paper *Completing the Internal Market*, the Commission drew attention to the possibility that increased mobility of resources could widen the existing regional disparities in the Community. This concern was strongly expressed by several member states, including Ireland, and is reflected in the Single Act in the form of new Treaty articles dealing with 'Economic and Social Cohesion'. These articles state that Community action should strengthen its economic and social cohesion and, in particular, would aim at reducing disparities between regions and the backwardness of the least favoured regions (Article 130A). The Act specified, in a general way, the means by which these objectives would be pursued. It states that both national and Community policy would further them and the Community would support their achievement through the

Structural Funds. It was also laid down that in implementing common or Community policies, including the internal market, account would be taken of the objectives of economic and social cohesion and convergence (Article 130B).

PART II

The Impact of EC Membership

The Possible Effects of Integration

How has membership of the European Community affected Ireland since 1973? The kinds of effects which are likely or possible are identified by examining theories of economic integration and existing studies of the effects of economic integration on other countries.

From these sources we can identify some of the likely effects of Ireland's membership of the EC.

- The most obvious effect of removing tariffs between countries is to alter the amount and pattern of trade.
- If the amount and pattern of trade between countries changes it is likely that the structure of production and employment in each country will also change.
- These changes in the pattern of trade, production and employment constitute the process of *specialisation* brought about by the freeing of international trade.
- Membership of the EC may also affect the efficiency of firms. In particular the removal of protective tariffs is likely to expose inefficient firms to severe competition. When firms respond to this by improving the efficiency with which they operate this is often called the 'cold shower effect' of integration.
- Economic integration can affect not only the kind of goods produced but also the structure of the firms and industries which produce them. One very important proposition is that reduction of barriers to trade will bring about an increase in concentration of industry. The idea is that access to foreign markets will increase the incentives for large-scale producers in each country to drive out marginal producers by increasing capacity and thereby lowering costs.

One of the major purposes of the Council's work on Ireland in the EC was to ascertain which of these effects has occurred in practice and which has been the most significant. To do this it was necessary to consider various indicators of performance since 1973. However, a study of the facts alone will not reveal what effects membership of the EC had on Ireland. The reason is that the facts of economic performance since 1973 were the result, not just of Ireland's integration into the European economy, but of a host of other factors also - such as trends in the world economy, technical change and economic policies adopted by Irish governments. This problem of identifying cause and effect is particularly acute in the case in hand. The reason is that Ireland's accession to the EC in 1973 coincided with a major and prolonged change in the world economic climate, resulting from international monetary instability and the oil crisis. Before attempting to identify the effects of integration, it is useful to first examine overall economic performance since 1973 both in itself and also by comparison with the other countries of the Community.

The Irish Economy in the European Community

THE IRISH ECONOMY SINCE 1973

Membership of the Community involved the gradual elimination of all protective tariffs or quotas on *manufactured* goods. However, international trade in *services* remained restricted by national regulations and standards. Agriculture was governed by a special regime known as the Common Agricultural Policy (CAP). When Ireland joined the EC it was agreed that Community rules would be applied gradually over a five year transition period from 1973 to 1978.

In assessing performance it is, therefore, appropriate to consider the transition phase separately. In addition, one of the striking differences between Ireland's economic performance since 1973 and that of other EC countries was the timing of phases of growth and recession. On the criteria of output, consumption, and employment, Ireland did better than the average from 1973 to 1980 and considerably worse than the average after 1980. Consequently, when interpreting events since 1973, with a view to assessing the effects of integration, we initially examine these two periods separately.

1. Economic Performance 1973-80

During this period the Irish economy grew faster than other Community countries and this was associated with rapid growth of both consumption and, especially, investment. Trends in employment and unemployment also compared favourably with other EC countries, and manufactured output grew faster than average. Turning from real to financial indicators, Ireland's experience was not so strong. Both inflation and the balance of payments deficit were high by EC standards - as was the growth of public sector deficits and public debt. Finally, Ireland's cost competitiveness in manufacturing industry (as measured by movements in hourly earnings and the nominal exchange rate) deteriorated steadily in relation to the UK, improved relative to most other EC countries, and deteriorated slightly relative to Ireland's main trading partners as a group.

2. Economic Performance 1980-86

This period was one of great difficulty for the Irish economy. Economic growth was lower in Ireland than in other EC countries and this was exacerbated by sharply increased financial outflows. As a result consumption grew very little indeed - though total investment growth was higher than elsewhere in the Community. The contraction of total employment in Ireland was well above the average and this contraction was heavily concentrated in industry. At the same time employment in services grew - but much less than in other Community countries. In addition, the Irish labour force grew very rapidly by European standards - because of the unusual demographic characteristics of Ireland. As a result of these trends, unemployment in Ireland increased substantially more than in the EC in general. Industrial production grew by a relatively small amount - except in those sectors dominated by new foreign-owned firms.

Developments in inflation, the balance of payments and the public finances were also distinctive in the period 1980 to 1986. In the early years of the period Irish inflation was far higher than the EC average and, for the first time, a very large difference between the Irish and the UK rate emerged. In the second half of the period there was a rapid disinflation and a most remarkable balance of payments adjustment - such that by 1988 inflation was below both the EC average and the UK rate. This adjustment was not reflected in the public finances for a number of reasons. Finally, the cost competitiveness of Irish manufacturing (as measured by movements in relative earnings and the nominal exchange rate) deteriorated considerably relative to that of other countries in the European Monetary System for most of the period. Competitiveness versus UK manufacturing increased in the early years of the period, and then decreased sharply - mainly as a result of movements of sterling on the foreign exchange markets.

Since 1987 the Irish economy has begun to perform in line with other Community countries and this can be identified as a third phase, or at least the first signs of a third phase of Ireland's experience in the Community.

IRELAND'S RELATIVE PERFORMANCE IN THE EC

An important part of the NESC's study of Ireland's membership of the EC consists of comparison of economic developments in Ireland with those in other member states and some non-EC countries. This approach allows us to distinguish trends which were common to all or some countries from those which were unique to Ireland. This helps in identifying the relative impact of the various forces at work since Ireland joined the Community.

1. Population and Labour Force

Ireland's population and labour force differ in important respects from those in most other EC countries. Ireland has:

- the lowest population density;
- the highest birth rate;
- the highest rate of natural population increase;
- the only significant rate of emigration;
- the highest dependency ratios;
- the second highest unemployment rate.

2. Income Levels and Standards of Living

Figure 1 shows the Commission's estimate of Gross Domestic Product (GDP) per head in each member country.

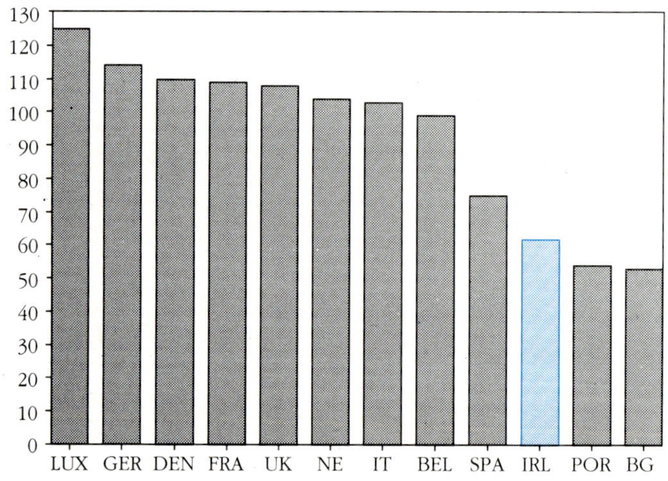

This shows that Ireland's GDP per head is 62.4% of the EC average. This figure probably overestimates Ireland's actual position - which may be nearer to 56% of the EC average - only slightly ahead of Greece and Portugal.

3. Trends in Relative Income and Economic Growth

Since 1973 Irish income per head has not increased significantly as a percentage of the Community average. Other countries have experienced much more dramatic changes in their relative income position.

In general, it is possible to identify two phases in the evolution of national incomes per head in Europe. From 1960 to around 1973/74 there was an unmistakable process of convergence; since the mid-seventies there has been a reversal. Ireland was something of an exception to this trend. Ireland did not participate in the convergence process during the first period (1960-73) but did start catching up between 1973 and 1980.

Indeed, since joining the Community there have been two periods when Ireland's growth has differed substantially from other European economies: in the period 1973 to 1980 the Irish economy grew more rapidly than other Community and European economies. From 1980 to 1986 Ireland experienced much slower growth than other countries. It is clear that Ireland's overall economic performance – as measured by economic growth, employment and unemployment - was much worse in the 1980s than the 1970s. It is possible to explain a part of this difference by reference to international developments and domestic economic policies. However, an important finding of the NESC's study is that, despite the stark contrast between Ireland's experience in the 1970s and the 1980s, *the effects of Ireland's integration into the EC* were not very different in these two decades. Consequently, when studying these effects, less emphasis should be put on the differences between the 1970s and the 1980s. Indeed, there are a number of distinct continuities between the two periods. When these are identified three things emerge:

(i) the economic performance in the seventies was not as strong as it might appear at first sight;
(ii) the poor performance for most of the eighties was related in a number of ways to economic developments in the seventies;
(iii) the problems in the economy cannot be fully explained by reference to the macroeconomic mismanagement which undoubtedly occurred in the late seventies and early eighties. Indeed, to some extent there are links between the fiscal crisis of this period and the long-run structural weaknesses of the Irish economy.

Conclusions on the Impact of EC Membership

IRELAND'S TRADE

As expected, membership of the EC had significant effects on Ireland's pattern of international trade. In many respects changes after 1973 were a continuation of trends observed from 1958 to 1972:

- Dependence on the UK market, as an outlet for Ireland's exports, decreased dramatically;
- Ireland's exports to both EC and non EC countries increased considerably;
- The value of food, drink and tobacco exports was soon overtaken by the value of other manufactured exports;
- Within manufactured exports, chemicals and machinery increased their share enormously;
- Increased manufactured exports, especially of chemicals and electronic machinery, have to a large extent been matched by increased imports of materials and components for these industries.

The greatest effects of EC membership were undoubtedly felt in manufacturing industry and in agriculture. Manufacturing industry was particularly influenced because barriers to trade in industrial goods were removed much more than barriers to trade in services.

MANUFACTURING INDUSTRY IN THE EC

Despite the apparent difference in economic performance in the two periods mentioned above, there were important factors common to both periods. First, there can be no doubt that much of the stagnation of the eighties was directly related to the need to correct the public sector and balance of payments deficits of the late seventies.

Second, our study of trends in employment, output, industrial structure and trade strongly indicate a process of *specialisation* and adjustment in the Irish economy - which occurred *continuously* once protection was removed. This process consisted of Ireland's specialisation *out* of a long list of exposed manufacturing industries, and their continual replacement by foreign firms in a narrow range of manufacturing activities (see panels). This pattern of adjustment *between* industries differs from that found in most other EC countries in the initial stages of integration. The development of the Community and, indeed, the growth of trade in the post-war period, has, in general, been characterised by specialisation *within* industries.

Third, this adjustment between industries has coincided with a significant alteration of the size-structure of indigenous manufacturing industry. Many of the industries which Ireland has specialised out of were those internationally-traded sectors in which larger Irish producers were once found. At the same time, much of the employment growth in manufacturing was in small-scale activities which benefit from an element of natural protection, because they serve very local markets. This is an important finding given the prediction, which has been confirmed in several other Community countries, that integration will stimulate a process of *concentration* - in which larger producers will eliminate their small domestic rivals in order to exploit the advantages of large scale available once access to a wider international market is provided by Community membership.

Thus, what may have seemed like a substantial adjustment and specialisation *within* industries in the seventies, taking a longer view, turned out to be a slow and somewhat delayed adjustment process in which Ireland was specialised *out of* many industries - especially those where innovative activity and scale are significant.

INDUSTRIES GROWING SINCE THE FREEING OF TRADE

Foreign-owned, grant-aided, export-oriented firms

Pharmaceuticals

Chemicals

Electronic and data processing equipment

Instrument engineering.

INDUSTRIES DECLINING SINCE THE FREEING OF TRADE

Internationally Traded, Relatively large scale

Textiles

Clothing

Footwear

Leather

Chemicals (parts of)

Motor vehicles and parts

Electrical engineering (parts of)

Shipbuilding

Bread, biscuits and flour confectionery

Sugar, cocoa, chocolate

Fruit and vegetable processing.

INDUSTRIES WHICH GROW WHEN DOMESTIC DEMAND GROWS AND DECLINE WHEN IT DECLINES

These are of two types:

Large Scale

Paper and printing

Drink and Tobacco

Food (parts of)

Non-metallic minerals.

Fragmented

Metal articles

Mechanical engineering

Electrical engineering (parts of)

Wood and furniture.

Interpreting the Experience of Irish Manufacturing

It is possible to interpret the entire experience of manufacturing, since accession, in terms of the response of firms to economic integration. The most immediate effect of economic integration was almost certainly the 'cold shower' effect. There can be little doubt that the removal of inefficient practices accounted for some of the rationalisation observed in the period after accession. Where job losses reflected improved efficiency, in response to the shock of competition, then firms could produce the same output at lower cost and would, indeed, have improved their position. The next effect of integration on firms is likely to have been specialisation on particular products *within* their own industry. Indeed, the message of much of the literature on the growth of trade following the formation of the EC, is that this specialisation *within* the industry often *completes* the process of adjustment.

But if the firms' basic scale was too small relative to their competitors, or if they suffered other competitive disadvantages, (both of which seem to be true of Irish manufacturing industry in the seventies), then the breathing space offered by removal of inefficiency, and by an element of specialisation on particular products, would only have been temporary. Consequently, competitive pressure for further adjustment inevitably built up. Where this further pressure forced contraction of output and employment, the adjustment to intensified international competition tended to become the process of long-run decline, inherent in international specialisation *between* industries. The reason was that, in industries where economies of scale existed, contractions of employment (except where they remove basic inefficiency or introduce new technologies), and contraction of output, tended to *raise* costs rather than *lower* them. Consequently, such 'adjustments', rather than re-establishing competitiveness on a new basis, were the start of a process of attrition. What we observed in the eighties was precisely *further* contraction or elimination of many of the indigenous firms in exposed and relatively large scale activities. Thus, the experience of Irish manufacturing industry since accession can be seen to be consistent with a sophisticated and realistic understanding of how trade and integration can work where there are initial differences in level of development, technology and scale of production. The analysis of the Irish experience in these terms suggests that some of the severe problems of manufacturing industry in Ireland in the period 1980 to 1986 should be seen as effects of economic integration, unredressed by counteracting policies.

In the period after 1973 increased basic efficiency, an element of specialisation within industries, a very buoyant home market, and devaluation of sterling, slowed the adjustment between industries - in Ireland's case, the run-down of most indigenous firms in relatively large-scale traded activities. But factors capable of reversing that adjustment were not found.

This leads to two general conclusions concerning the experience of manufacturing in Ireland in the whole period since accession to the European Community. First, in the case of Ireland, the adjustment to integration has involved considerably more than increased efficiency, resulting from the shock of international competition, and specialisation on particular products *within* each industry. It seems to also have effected a very substantial rearrangement of the pattern of manufacturing activity undertaken in Ireland. Second, the overall experience since 1973 seems, unfortunately, to confirm the accuracy of the observation that for smaller EC countries, scale-driven exports (within and without the EC) are vital for international competitiveness in many industries.

IRISH AGRICULTURE IN THE EC

A major reason for Ireland's membership of the EC was the desire to achieve access to a large and regulated market for agricultural output. Access to this market did indeed yield strongly rising real farm incomes between 1974 and 1978. A number of factors then conspired to reverse this trend and Irish agricultural output and, especially, incomes fell back considerably. In recent years average incomes have recovered strongly.

1. Support from the Common Agricultural Policy

An important aspect of Ireland's membership of the Community since 1973 is the support which the CAP provides to the country as a whole. The level of transfers to any member state of the Community can only be defined and calculated by reference to some alternative policy arrangement. This means that several different calculations of CAP transfers to Ireland can validly be made. Despite this it can be said that total CAP support to Ireland has varied between 5% and 10% of GNP.

2. Problems in the Agricultural Sector

In our study of the experience since Ireland joined the EC we identified three problems in the agricultural sector:

(i) The reversal between 1978 and 1986 of the progress in incomes made between 1973 and 1978;

(ii) The persistence of very low and volatile farm incomes for a sizeable segment of Irish farmers;

(iii) The slow rate of development of the food industry;

The persistence of these problems despite the receipt of very substantial support from the CAP indicates that in some way the constraints on the development of Irish agriculture have not been fully removed by the Common Agricultural Policy.

3. Reversal of Income Growth

The strong progress made in average farm incomes between 1972 and 1978 was reversed after 1978, and a significant upward trend was resumed only after 1986. Although many factors were involved, these events can be attributed to two broad developments. The first was the continuation of Ireland's high inflation rate, compared to that of other member states, in the years following the formation of the EMS. The major explanation which suggests itself was pursuit of domestic fiscal and monetary policies which were not consistent with the exchange rate policy inherent in EMS membership. The second, and related reason, was the moderation of common EC price increases. Together these worked to create a very severe price-cost squeeze on Irish farmers. Irish farmers experienced the greatest decrease in 'real' prices in the Community between 1978 and 1985.

4. Low Farm Incomes

The increased output of Irish agriculture in the seventies and eighties was provided by a minority, perhaps 25 to 30%, of farms. The persistence of a sizeable segment of Irish agriculture showing very low farm incomes is related to the continued existence of severe structural problems which inhibit the response to the strong incentives offered by the CAP. Throughout the seventies, as in earlier decades, there was indeed a steady reduction of the number at work in agriculture. However, it is striking that despite this outflow, the number of farms decreased very little and thus, as in the manufacturing sector, the adjustment which did take place did not solve the structural problems.

Not only could these problems not be solved by the CAP but they may have been exacerbated by it. This implies that these structural problems, if they were to be solved, should have been the subject of national policy. But *national* agricultural policy has failed to tackle effectively the problems arising from the structure of land tenure and transfer.

5. Slow Development of the Food Industry

The development of the food processing industry has been seriously constrained by the availability of supply and the seasonality of production. This relates both to the CAP and the structural problems of Irish agriculture. While the CAP was not the original cause of these features it would seem to have inadvertently reinforced them by the incentives it created to achieve income, production and stabilisation objectives. In contrast with the structural problems, it is less easy to see that *national* policy could have *directly* altered the set of incentives facing producers and processors - since they emanated largely from the CAP. However, if a strategic emphasis on the development of an industrial sector based on agricultural produce had been adopted earlier, measures might have been taken under industrial or regional policy, and the problematic aspects of the CAP could have been given priority in Ireland's negotiations at Community level.

6. Conclusion on Agriculture

In conclusion, while the CAP has supported increased farm incomes for some, it has not overcome, and may even have exacerbated, two fundamental problems in Irish agriculture: the persistence of low farm incomes for a considerable number of farmers and the slow development of the food industry. Both problems relate to the continuation of severe structural problems - despite a substantial reduction of numbers involved in agriculture.

CONCLUSIONS

1. The Effects of EC Membership

The most significant impact of Ireland's membership of the Community has been on manufacturing industry and agriculture. The conventional approach to assessing the effects of EC membership has concentrated on job losses and exports in manufacturing and CAP transfers in agriculture. The approach taken in this Report is different in that it considers not only the levels of income, employment and exports but also the *structures* which were created or preserved as a result of EC and national policy. Under this approach the criterion by which Ireland's membership of the Community should be assessed is primarily the *kind of economy* which evolved as a result of EC membership and only secondarily whether a particular strategy maximised gross exports or receipts from the Commission.

Integration into the European economy not only caused the loss of certain jobs in indigenous manufacturing - as is widely acknowledged - but also brought about significant changes in the structure of indigenous manufacturing industry. In particular, it eliminated many relatively large indigenous firms in internationally traded activities. This change in structure undermined the leading firms in industries where innovative activity or scale are significant and thus reduced the ability of indigenous manufacturing to generate industrial growth. The failure of indigenous industrialisation has correctly been identified as one of the major long run structural weaknesses of the Irish economy.

As has been indicated in the conclusion on agriculture, severe structural problems remained despite a substantial reduction of numbers involved in agriculture. The major difference between Ireland's industrial and agricultural sectors in the EC has been that the Community system made adjustment in industry unavoidable, whereas in agriculture it made adjustment partially avoidable, while at the same time rewarding the strong far more lavishly than the weak. This system could conceal the need for a range of long-term national policies concerning the role of agriculture in the development of the economy.

Despite the difference between the Community regimes for industry and agriculture, there is a certain parallel between what happened in Irish industry and agriculture. Painful adjustments occurred in each sector, to a greater or lesser extent; but those adjustments did not solve the structural problems of either industry or agriculture. Consequently, further adjustment, of the same sort, was inevitably necessary.

In summary, the very pronounced specialisation which has occurred in the Irish economy since accession has not provided a foundation for indigenous economic development.

2. Assessing EC Membership

The developments since 1973 documented in the NESC report have led some commentators to infer that the report shows that EC membership was harmful to the Irish economy. We want to stress that no such inference can validly be made. In fact there can be little doubt that membership of the Community was better for Ireland than non-membership would have been. Three considerations underly this statement:

(i) it is based on a realistic assessment of the policies which would be available to Ireland if she were outside the EC and on appreciation of the external economic forces which would still operate;

(ii) only a portion of the economic problems documented in our report can be seen as the effects of economic integration.

This report, and several earlier NESC reports, have also identified major failures in Irish policy making. It cannot be said that Ireland adopted the policies it did or, more accurately, failed to develop policies, *because of its membership of the EC*. Consequently, it cannot be argued that Irish policy making would have been better if Ireland had remained outside the Community;

(iii) EC membership has brought to light fundamental weaknesses in the Irish economy, but it cannot be said that membership of the Community was the *cause* of these structural problems. To see this one need only recall the economic and social crisis experienced in the 1950s - under a regime of industrial protection. It is these structural weaknesses which must now be addressed by both national and Community policy.

Lessons of the Period 1973 - 87

Part II of the report concluded with a statement of a number of lessons drawn by the Council from its analysis of Ireland's experience in the Community to date (see Chapter 7). We summarise these here.

(i) Domestic macroeconomic policy did not take sufficient account of the greatly increased interdependence of Ireland and other EC economies.

(ii) Domestic macroeconomic policy was, for a considerable period, inconsistent with the decision to join the EMS. Successful membership of the EMS required not only a correct macroeconomic approach but a high degree of consensus on earnings and taxation.

(iii) The reduction in the macroeconomic policy autonomy of the member states, which was an unavoidable implication of economic integration, has not been adequately replaced by Community level responsibility for the management of the macroeconomy.

(iv) Although the commitment of Ireland to Community membership was very strong, this was not matched by detailed appreciation of the likely effects of economic integration. In particular, it was not appreciated that the effects of integration can take considerable time to work themselves out. Adjustments to membership of the EC were experienced in the 1980s as well as the 1970s.

(v) The greatest single difference between the regime of protection, such as that which prevailed in Ireland for several decades, and membership of the Community is the necessity for *specialisation* in a free trade environment. Ireland did not immediately set about identifying fields in which she could *specialise* on the basis of genuine, sustainable and renewable competitive advantages. The very pronounced specialisation which did occur, did not provide a foundation for indigenous economic development.

(vi) Economic integration does not, of itself, bring about regional convergence. Indeed, it tends to reflect and reinforce existing regional advantages and disadvantages. This fact was not adequately understood by the Community - as shown by the underdeveloped state of the Community's structural and redistributive policies.

(vii) The development policies pursued by Irish governments did not sufficiently, consistently or systematically address the key structural constraints on Irish economic development. It is important that this factor is kept in mind when considering the divergences from average European growth in the late seventies and eighties. It is this which provides the link between what is known, and agreed, about weaknesses in macro-management, and what is known, partly as a result of NESC's work, about the long-run structural weaknesses of the Irish economy.

(viii) During much of the period since Ireland's accession to the EC, priority was given to *short-term* goals by both government and society.

(ix) The balance between national and Community policy has not always been correct. In some cases, such as agriculture, the existence of a Community policy was seen as virtually precluding national policy. In other cases, for example regional policy, an increased Commission role was viewed with ambivalence - but not on the basis of a superior national grasp of regional development planning.

(x) Membership of the European Community increases rather than reduces the need for clear Irish policy aims and methods.

PART III

1992: Threats and Opportunities

A Framework for Analysis

THE IMPACT OF 1992

The internal market programme involves the removal of all obstacles to the movement of goods, services and capital arising from non-tariff barriers (NTBs). These NTBs arise from national customs checks, national technical standards, national aids to industry, national public procurement, national professional qualifications and national company law. The programme involves the passing of Community law governing all these areas.

The 300 measures listed in the Commission's White Paper *Completing the Internal Market* have three immediate economic objectives. They aim to facilitate trade by reducing the obstacles to the efficient and economical distribution of goods within the EC. They intend to eliminate many of the non-tariff barriers to trade and thereby increase market access and reduce the segmentation of the market. Finally, they plan to liberalise public procurement practices which should also reduce market segmentation.

1. Direct Effects of Market Completion

Completion of the internal market will have both direct and indirect effects. Indeed, two distinct *direct* effects can be identified.

Cost *reduction* will result from removal of non-tariff barriers (NTBs). For example, firms should be able to find cheaper inputs; transport, insurance, packaging and labelling costs should fall and the overall cost of goods traded should be reduced by the removal of bureaucratic obstacles. These cost reductions should help to reduce prices and, consequently, increase demand and output.

Increased competition will result from the improved market access of firms in all countries. Firms which currently operate high price-cost margins or price discrimination should find this ability curtailed by increased competition. In short, firms will find it less easy to practice market segmentation. In addition, measures such as the liberalisation of public procurement should encourage market entry by other EC producers and, consequently, increased competition.

The relative strength of these two direct effects will differ from industry to industry. It is, however, possible to identify some of the factors which determine the strength of the two direct effects.

Cost Reduction

The extent of immediate cost reduction clearly depends on the height of NTBs in different industries. Some NTBs affect all industries which produce tradable products - the most obvious example being customs costs. Others affect only some industries - for example, national packaging, labelling or technical standards and national government procurement practices. It is agreed that, in general, NTBs are relatively less important in low-technology products than in high-technology markets. But customs delays or road transport quotas may impose a much greater cost penalty on low-technology products since they will form a higher proportion of the value of the product.

Increased Competition

Price reductions resulting directly from increased competition will depend upon the current degree of concentration of an industry. Industries such as textiles, clothing and footwear are already highly competitive. By contrast, other industries, such as pharmaceuticals, man-made fibres, office machinery, domestic electrical appliances and motor vehicles are highly concentrated, or market entry is restricted, and firms in individual national markets have scope for monopoly pricing, price discrimination and inefficiencies.

2. Indirect Effects of Market Completion

These two direct effects may be the start of the two chains of causation which create substantial *indirect* effects. These can be labelled 'size' and 'competition' and are depicted schematically in Figure 6.1

FIGURE 6.1

The Two Channels of Direct and Indirect Effects of Market Completion

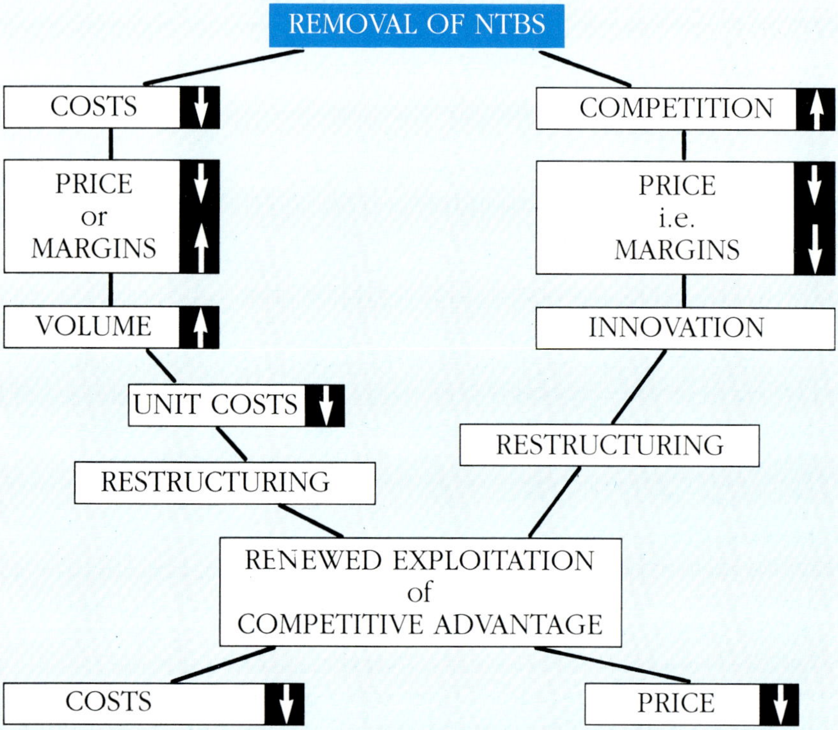

Market Size

The *direct* effect of removal of NTBs may be to reduce costs and, consequently, price. As the quantity demanded and supplied increases, the firm may find costs of production falling again because of *economies of scale*. This promotes further price reductions and output growth. There are, however, other indirect effects. The process of increasing output and exploiting economies of scale involves larger, low-cost, producers eliminating smaller high-cost firms and can, consequently, initiate a major *restructuring* of industry - in particular, but not only, rationalisation. This is a very important possible indirect effect of market completion.

Competition and Innovation
Increased competition is likely to have a positive impact on technical progress and the diffusion of innovation. This is at variance with a traditional idea that monopoly, despite its attendant costs, was more conducive to R+D and innovation. The new view denies that large firm *size* is conducive to innovation and argues instead that rapid market *growth* strongly stimulates innovation in industry.

It is argued that firms faced with more aggressive competition will seek not only to *match* the competition, by cost reductions, but also to *evade* it by repositioning themselves. They can do this by *differentiating* their product from that of their rivals. Product differentiation usually requires innovation of some sort and so completion of the internal market will induce firms to innovate. This view leads to the expectation that completion of the market, by increasing competition, will have a major dynamic impact on those sectors in which current NTBs are high, technological development is significant, and the outlook for market growth is good. Clearly this dynamic process would initially be much stronger in some sectors than in others.

Conclusions on Direct and Indirect Effects
In using this framework for analysis there are two propositions which are significant. First, the indirect effects of market completion are likely to be more substantial than the direct effects. Second, and most important, the relative size and nature of the direct and indirect effects will differ between sectors of the economy. Consequently, detailed analysis of individual sectors is required.

Firm Size in the Internal Market
There is a clear tension between the view that further concentration of industry is likely (because significant economies of scale remain to be exploited) and the view that the larger market will increase the *variety* of products available, and hence that small and medium sized enterprises will benefit most (because they currently suffer most from non-tariff barriers and, most importantly, because they have the characteristics, in particular, the ability to innovate, which are most important for success in a unified internal market).

This issue is important for Ireland because - as revealed in our analysis of the changes in the manufacturing sector since accession - very few large-scale internationally-traded activities undertaken by indigenous firms have survived Ireland's integration into the European economy. If a substantial part of the increased competition created by completion of the market was to take the form of cost reduction based on scale expansion, then the fear naturally arises that Irish firms would find it very difficult to compete. Furthermore, if completion implies increased firm size, then *barriers to entry* of various sorts may increase - even though market completion also means increased competition *between these dominant firms* in a given industry. If, on the other hand, those who stress competition and innovation are correct, then the increased competition resulting from market completion will be based only to a small extent on exploitation of scale economies and will take a number of other forms such as technological activity aimed at product and process development, product differentiation, market segmentation, and redefinition of firms' specialisation. It might be concluded that in this case the prospects for Irish firms are better.

The argument between these two views turns on a number of theoretical and empirical points and, given the significance of the issue, the Council felt it necessary to examine them in some detail. Having considered all the relevant arguments, the Council is inclined to the conclusion that economies of scale remain relevant and will play a significant part in the competitive response to completion of the internal market.

This conclusion does not deny the validity of the view that 1992 will stimulate innovation, but it does affect the implications of that view. If there are any significant advantages of scale, then, in their attempt to survive, small firms are constrained to adopt very particular strategies. For example, small or medium sized firms can prosper so long as they can acquire some competitive advantage over their bigger rivals. One frequently cited advantage is the ability to respond more rapidly to change. Indeed, the innovativeness of small and medium sized firms, highlighted by those who stress the second channel of causation, is a perfect example of this. But a strategy of being more innovative than larger competitors is a highly *demanding* one; it requires considerable management ability, technical skills and, probably, technology.

Consequently, an internal market with increased competition stimulating innovation by small and medium sized firms, may be *different* from increased competition based on scale economies, but may be only marginally less difficult for Irish firms.

The Manufacturing Sector

'1992' AND THE CHANGING ECONOMIC ENVIRONMENT

One of the most important points to emerge from the analysis is that 1992 must be seen in the context of other changes in the general economic environment affecting businesses. The important aspects of the general economic environment are technical change, organisational change, macroeconomic conditions and the emergence of important new producers, in particular from Japan and the newly industrialised countries. The most important of these is the phenomenal wave of technical change which is sweeping the world economy. The importance of technical and organisational change was confirmed when we applied our framework for analysis to Irish manufacturing industry. In several sectors the dominant threats and opportunities were created by technical and organisational change rather than the removal of non-tariff barriers.

Given the connection between 1992 and the autonomous changes in the world economy, a fairly broad view is adopted when assessing the threats and opportunities facing Irish firms. Thus it is considered appropriate to mention threats and opportunities which arise from technical or other business developments. However, as far as possible, we have identified whether a particular threat or opportunity is a direct result of market completion or not.

THREATS AND OPPORTUNITIES FACING IRISH MANUFACTURING INDUSTRY

Most manufacturing sectors in Ireland are hindered rather than helped by the sort of non-tariff barriers which fragment the European market. The clearest examples are the extra costs imposed by customs checks and the imposition of national technical standards. The first falls heavily on Irish manufacturers because a high proportion of their output is exported, and access to European markets can involve crossing several borders. Indeed, some commentators on 1992 have generalised this and concluded that small countries will gain most from completion of the market because a higher proportion of their production is traded.

However, given this general observation that there are few non-tariff barriers protecting Irish manufacturing industry, it is important to think clearly about how this will translate into threats and opportunities after 1992. The completion of the internal market can benefit a firm only by lowering costs and giving it access to markets from which it was previously excluded.

Application of our analytical framework to manufacturing industry revealed that the *direct* effects of market completion are likely to be positive for most sectors. Possible threats came to light when the *indirect* effects were considered and when other factors like technical change were taken into account. The following is a brief summary of the implications for individual sectors.

- In the food processing sector the small scale of the Irish businesses relative to their European and especially US competitors was identified as a possible cause for concern.
- In electronics existing plants and the future flow of foreign direct investment were considered separately. Existing producers should find the *direct* effects beneficial, but these are likely to be small relative to the indirect effects. However, in this industry the *indirect* effects are very difficult to predict since they depend as much on firms' strategies, as on economic conditions. The flow of new foreign investment to Ireland is likewise hard to predict. While foreign direct investment in Europe certainly seems to be reviving, Ireland will experience increasing competition from new member states Greece, Spain and Portugal and from countries with large home markets, such as the UK.
- In electrical engineering a threat exists because large firms, both European and non-European, seem likely to reduce the number of plants they operate in Europe and this process contains potential dangers.
- In metal articles and mechanical engineering, technical change presents a possible threat to Irish producers; current trends in technology allow large producers to meet highly specialised needs with differentiated products.

- The processing of metals may be threatened by changes in the Community steel regime.
- In the automotive components sector, possible threats arise from the impact of technical and organisational change on the location of plants supplying the major motor manufacturers.
- Clothing is one sector where the *direct* effects of market completion may not be positive because, unlike most other industries, producers in other member states receive little extra protection from non-tariff barriers. In addition, the indirect effects of market completion may contain threats since the technical and organisational requirements for competitive success will be more easily acquired by larger firms.
- In textiles what threats exist seem to arise from the high and rising capital costs which are created by technical change. This tends to give large and well capitalised companies an advantage over others.
- Printing and publishing is a sector in which threats arise for different parts of the industry from technical change and from economies of scale.
- In chemicals, 1992 seems likely to create few threats and few opportunities.
- In pharmaceuticals a vigorous completion of the internal market would probably cause a radical restructuring of the industry in a direction which could, on balance, favour Ireland. However, it is unlikely that the segmentation of the European market will be undermined by 1992.

These threats do not define the inevitable outcome of completion of the internal market for two very important reasons. First, as well as threats there are considerable opportunities - as indicated by the generally beneficial *direct* effects of market completion which we expect. Second, many of the threats outlined above can be overcome, and the opportunities seized, if the correct corporate and public policy response can be devised. But these responses require realistic analysis of the process of economic integration and other processes of economic change, which must then be applied to each industry by those who know and understand the industry.

The Services Sector

INTRODUCTION

Completion of the internal market has three main components: the removal of physical, technical and fiscal barriers within the Community. The removal of technical barriers covers the free movement of goods, the free movement of labour and the professions, liberalisation of capital movements, the opening up of public procurement and the creation of a common market for services.

The Commission argues that the establishment of a common market in services is one of the main preconditions for a return to economic prosperity. The importance of the sector derives from the growing contribution of market and non-market services in total value-added and employment in the Community. The Commission suggests opening up the whole internal market for services, covering new service areas such as information, marketing and audiovisual services and the traditional services such as transport, banking and insurance.

IMPLICATIONS OF MARKET COMPLETION

The effects of market completion *per se* are likely to be much more prevalent in the services sector than in the manufacturing sector. This is because international market penetration in services is quite low by comparison with international trade in goods. In some cases this arises because the service can only be provided on the spot. However, one of the main reasons is the continuing existence of barriers to trade in services throughout the Community. In effect, therefore, many service sectors will now face what the manufacturing sector faced in 1973, when Ireland joined the Community.

1. Transport

In the case of transport, the opening up of the market requires:

(i) the phasing out of quantitative restrictions (quotas) for the transport of goods by road between member states, and the establishment of conditions under which non-resident carriers may operate transport services in another member state;

(ii) freedom to provide services for the transport of passengers by road;

(iii) greater freedom in air transport services, in particular, changing the system for the setting and approval of fares and limiting the rights of governments to restrict capacity and access to the market.

In terms of road haulage all quantitative restrictions on the operation and movement of vehicles are to be abolished by 1 January 1993. Liberalisation will also involve the introduciton of cabotage operations (point to point haulage within one state by the resident of another). The increase in competition implied by these changes will undoubtedly reduce the cost to users of haulage services. It will provide a challenge to Irish hauliers since foreign firms will be able to compete for their business.

In moving to a more liberalised air transport regime three main areas are affected - tariffs, capacity controls and access to the market. The EC made considerable progress towards the introduction of a more liberalised regime in 1987, including the application of the competition rules of the Treaty of Rome to civil aviation.

In spite of the liberalisation measures adopted in 1987, protection of carriers from open market conditions by member states is still possible. For example, there exists an EC regulation which permits a government to intervene and prohibit capacity increases where the share of its flag carrier has fallen below 40 per cent. Other features of the EC's 1987 'liberalising' measures which could adversely affect Irish airlines operating Fifth-Freedom services (i.e. services between non-domestic destinations) are the limitation of sales to 30 per cent of capacity and the requirement that all flights must begin and end in Ireland. The removal of all these constraints should be a major objective of Irish policy in the next phase of negotiations due to begin in 1990.

2. Distribution

While the Commission has not made any specific proposals in relation to the distribution sector, its proposals in relation to tax approximation and the abolition of economic borders, together with changes in competition policy will have a major bearing on the evolution of that sector.

The absence of economic borders will permit consumers to shop unhindered in the various Community countries. Competition policy will have its impact through the regulation of exclusive distribution agreements and limitation on the scope for market segmentation and price discrimination

The major impact of these measures will be on importing/wholesaling. UK firms supplying the Irish market will find it considerably easier to dispense with agents and deliver direct to retailers. There may also be a trend to rationalise the distribution system on the island by appointing a single distributor covering the Republic and the North. The major factor making for change in this area is that an Irish importer will be unable, under EC competition policy, to prevent Irish retailers from going to the UK or elsewhere to obtain better terms. Economies of scale in importing means that a UK importer could be in a much stronger competitive position than his Irish counterpart. This, together with the absence of border formalities, will make the post-1992 situation radically different.

Businesses where after sales service is important may have some protection from these tendencies. For the retail sector, the initial impact of 1992 should be confined to a harmonisation of prices, without directly affecting profit margins. For consumers in the Republic, 1992 should mean some limited reduction in net-of-tax prices over and above the effects of tax approximation.

3. Financial Services

The major change proposed by the EC to open up the market for financial services is the concept of freedom of establishment and home country supervision. For banking this is to be achieved through the Second Banking Directive, so that a bank, once authorised in any member state will be free to do banking business in any other member state without additional authorisation in that state. The Home State licencing authority will be responsible for the authorisation and prudential supervision of that bank, wherever it operates in the Community. Acceptance of home state authorisation requires an EC role regarding minimum standards.

Similarly, transactions in unit trusts and equivalent products will only require home country authorisation and may be freely marketed within the EC. A further directive covers investment services in the securities field.

In the case of non-life insurance the Commission's proposals involve a liberal regime for large risks and a more stringent regime for mass risks (i.e. smaller type risks) with a continuing supervisory role for the regulatory authorities in the country where the insurance is being sought. A similar directive for life assurance is expected to provide freedom to sell life assurance across frontiers. Ireland, along with a number of other countries has been afforded special transitional arrangements regarding implementation of the directive.

In terms of the framework for analysis outlined earlier, the *direct* effects of financial market integration are likely to lead to price falls of at least the European average, given the degree of concentration in certain sub-sectors of the domestic financial services market. An EC-wide study has estimated that the prices of financial services are likely to fall by 10 per cent on average. In banking it is important to distinguish between retail and wholesale banking: international competition has been a feature of the wholesale market to a much greater extent than in the retail market. Since competition would not have been as strong in the retail market, price reductions there may be more significant. Institutions serving narrow segments of the financial services industry, such as building societies, have not previously faced such intensive international competition and may therefore face substantial adjustment pressures.

It is now necessary to consider the *indirect* effects specified in our framework for analysis. Were economies of scale to be very significant in the provision of financial services, then businesses with large home markets would be likely to have better cost structures than those with smaller domestic markets. The balance of evidence suggests that economies of scale are exhausted at relatively low size levels. In general, *efficiency* differences are a greater source of cost differences than size. Size *per se* is, therefore not a necessary condition for competitive success. Consequently, Irish institutions are not inherently disadvantaged by virtue of their small domestic market. This is not to say that competing in a unified market will not cause any difficulties; the conditions for success are outlined later under the responses to 1992. Again, in the case of specialist institutions serving narrow segments, such as building societies, economies of scale are much more significant, so that they may be more vulnerable to completion of the internal market.

Completion of the internal market also presents

opportunities. Since the Irish financial market has not been as protected as the financial sectors of certain other European countries, opportunities for penetrating these markets arise. Based on the EC-wide study of financial service prices, the new members of the Community in southern Europe are likely to be particularly appropriate targets. The recent EC Directives expand the options which are open to financial institutions penetrating foreign markets. These are also discussed later under corporate responses.

The Regional Impact

TENDENCIES FOR REGIONAL CONVERGENCE AND DIVERGENCE

The impact of completion of the internal market on the disparities between regions in the EC is crucial. Approaches to regional policy and to several other policy areas will differ depending on whether further integration of the European economy is expected to bring about convergence of regional economies or a widening of the already considerable gaps between regional incomes. In order to identify the regional effects of economic integration the Council has undertaken a detailed investigation of various theories which predict regional diffusion or concentration of economic activity and assessed their theoretical validity and realism.

1. Regional Convergence by Market Forces

Mainstream economic theory, based on the notion of the economy as a self-adjusting mechanism, formulates the regional dimension in a way which stresses the tendency to regional balance. According to this theory, the normal functioning of supply and demand will tend to achieve full utilisation of all resources within each region and, more significantly in the current context, tend to eliminate disparities between different regions. This theory of regional convergence is widely considered to be invalid since it is based on some highly unrealistic assumptions.

2. Forccs Making for Regional Concentration of Economic Activity

A much more promising approach to understanding the existence and persistence of regional inequalities is that which invokes the 'principle of cumulative causation'. If there are 'economies of scale in production' (the cost of production of goods falls as output increases) or if there are 'economies of agglomeration' (the cost of production is lower because of the proximity of other firms) then a region which gets an initial advantage will find that advantage reinforced as its level of production increases. Each time output is increased, costs fall and other regions find it more difficult to catch up. If the strong region attracts capital and labour from weaker regions, this will further enhance its productive potential and, because of the economies of scale and of agglomeration, strengthen its competitive advantage. Hence the label 'cumulative causation'; output growth, by lowering costs, developing skills and know-how, inducing innovation and specialisation, creates a self-sustaining growth process in certain regions; but other regions may find themselves in a cycle of decline. In this view, economic disparities, far from being self-adjusting, or self-correcting, as in the orthodox vision, tend to be *self-reinforcing*.

Other factors which reinforce the tendency to concentration can be added:

- economies of scale in provision of infrastructure
- advantageous labour market characteristics
- innovation leadership.

This formidable list of arguments would seem to justify the conclusion that there are considerable forces making for concentration of advanced economic activity.

In spite of strong tendencies to concentration of industrial and economic activity it would be very surprising if there were not also counter-tendencies. What tendencies towards diffusion can be identified, and are they sufficiently strong to counteract the forces making for concentration?

3. Forces for Diffusion of Manufacturing Industry

It is clear that since the second world war large corporations have chosen to locate different parts of their businesses in very different regions and countries. In particular, manufacturing plants have frequently been located in less developed and peripheral areas. In addition, many of the traditional industrial regions in advanced countries seem to have become 'de-industrialised'.

To this pressure for diffusion of certain industrial activities may be added the effect of improvements in transport and telecommunications infrastructure which reduce the significance of distance. Another factor limiting regional imbalances is the fact that rapid growth in central areas puts a strain on their infrastructure and creates congestion costs.

Assessment

Do these arguments warrant the conclusion that the forces of diffusion are such that the completion of the internal market may be expected to coincide with a narrowing of the disparities between rich and poor regions in Europe? In our judgement the answer must be: no. There are two reasons for reaching this conclusion. First, the diffusion of industry as a result of the 'new spatial division of labour' is not the only force influencing the pattern of regional development; some of the other forces at work, such as technical and organisational changes, tend to maintain or even reinforce concentration. Second, even where the new spatial division of labour is creating a diffusion of certain manufacturing activities, this diffusion is *not* likely to bring about convergence of regional incomes and economic structures.

EUROPEAN GROWTH AND REGIONAL CONVERGENCE

1. The Effects of Growth on Regional Disparities

Some people have argued that completion of the internal market will reduce regional disparities because it will increase the *growth* rate of the European economy *as a whole*. The view that rapid growth of the European economy is generally conducive to reduction in regional disparities almost certainly has some validity. However, we do not see it as capable of supporting the proposition that completion of the internal market will *of itself* start a process of regional income convergence.

One reason is that the relationship between high European growth in the period 1960-73 and an element of convergence of regional and national incomes in those years, on the one hand, and low growth in 1974-86 and slight divergence, on the other, has not been analysed in sufficient detail. From the simple correlation highlighted by the Commission, it is not possible to identify *how* EC growth affects national or regional growth. A research project on the scale of the 'Cecchini Report' would be required before knowledge of the nature and strength of the relationships involved could be confidently acquired.

THE 'CECCHINI REPORT' AND THE DISTRIBUTION OF GAINS FROM 1992

A different view of the likely regional distribution of gains from market completion can be found in what has become known as the 'Cecchini Report'. In the preparation of that report no attempt was made to estimate, or even to ascertain the broad orders of magnitude of the relative gains of different regions. Nevertheless,

Market Completion and Convergence: A General Conclusion

After considering all the arguments, our general conclusion must be that the benefits of market completion are likely to be unevenly distributed - with the greatest benefits accruing to regions in which industries with economies of scale and highly innovative sectors are most prevalent. Ireland is not such a region. Consequently, completion of the internal market of itself, should not be expected to narrow the income disparities between regions in the EC, let alone bring about convergence. This is a fundamental conclusion which informs the entire report.

in the 'Summary and Conclusion' it is stated that smaller and newer member states "have proportionately the biggest opportunities for gain from market integration" and it is clearly implied that the distribution of the gains, if uneven at all, is likely to favour these regions in these states. In the Council's, view the arguments developed by Cecchini to support these conclusions are erroneous and they should be seen, therefore, as no more than assertions.

Taxation and Integration

INDIRECT TAX APPROXIMATION AND INTEGRATION

The measures that need to be taken to unify the internal market come under the headings of physical, technical and fiscal barriers. The most obvious physical barriers are customs posts at frontiers. However, the presence of physical barriers is inextricably bound up with the technical and fiscal divisions between member states. Since completion of the internal market involves total elimination of frontier controls and checks, border tax adjustments will have to be either eliminated or reformed in ways that do not require border formalities. The Commission argues that once customs have been abolished it would be impossible to retain wide differences in VAT rates and excise duties. Indirect tax approximation is therefore a means to an end (removal of frontiers and customs posts), not an end in itself.

The Commission initially presented a set of proposals for indirect tax approximation in 1987. Revised proposals were subsequently issued in May 1989 (see panel).

The Council has assessed the Commission's proposals on tax approximation and the fiscal dimension of the European integration on four criteria: the tax requirements of economic integration, the principles of taxation underlying the package of tax reforms previously devised by the Council, the revenue gain or loss from implementing the proposals and the distributive implications.

In the Council's view, approximation of VAT rates is necessary for the removal of physical frontiers which is, in turn, necessary for the removal of obstacles to trade in the Community. Consequently, the Council supports the broad idea of VAT approximation. However, the Commission's revised proposals on VAT approximation do not accord well with the programme of domestic tax reform advocated by the Council. The revised proposals represent a distinct shift towards a 'market forces' approach, with the Commission confining itself to proposing minimum rates, and taxation systems being subsequently forced into alignment by virtue of market forces. In the Irish case market forces would manifest themselves most rapidly on the border with Northern Ireland. In this scenario it is likely that the Irish standard rate could not remain appreciably above 15 per cent, and rates much above zero on items zero-rated in the UK would be unsustainable. Under this arrangement the Irish exchequer would experience significant revenue losses with consequent effects on taxation and/or expenditure.

EC'S TAX PROPOSALS

Original Proposals

- A standard VAT rate of between 14 and 20 per cent.
- A reduced VAT rate of between 4 and 9 per cent.
- No provision for zero rates, with basic necessities to be charged at the reduced rate.
- Excise duties on tobacco products, mineral oils and alcohol to be uniform across the Community.

Revised Proposals

- A minimum standard VAT rate of 15 per cent.
- A reduced VAT rate of between 4 and 9 per cent.
- Zero rates allowed on a small number of products.
- Uniform excise duty rates to be replaced by bands or minimum tax rates (unspecified).

Community-wide approximation of excise duties on tobacco and alcohol is not necessary for the removal of frontiers; certain differences in rates can be retained, provided an alternative system of control, based on physical markings, is used. There are also sound economic and social reasons for retaining high excise duties on drink and tobacco in certain member states, including Ireland. Consequently, the Council supports the *broad thrust* of the Commission's *revised* proposals on excise duties in the sense of allowing greater flexibility. However, in order to minimise the costs arising from cross-border shopping some approximation of duties within different zones of the Community should be considered.

INTEGRATION AND DIRECT TAX REFORM

In devising Ireland's approach to indirect tax approximation account must be taken of other aspects of the Irish tax system and other implications of the completion of the internal market.

(a) As demonstrated in previous Council publications a major flaw in the direct tax system is the narrowness of the tax base and the related high income tax rates. The solution to this problem lies in the widening of the tax base (including the introduction of a property tax,and reduction of personal income tax.

(b) The significantly enhanced mobility of labour and capital, which will result from the completion of the internal market, will greatly increase the existing pressure for approximation of income and some other *direct* taxes in the EC, if distortionary tax-induced migration of labour and capital are to be minimised. One of the many anomalies of the existing Irish tax system is that it is biased towards taxation of *mobile* factors while *immobile* factors are treated very favourably.

Consequently, the current phase of European integration greatly increases the urgency of reforming the domestic tax system.

PUBLIC FINANCE IN ECONOMIC INTEGRATION

The Council felt it necessary to scrutinise the overall system of public finance of the EC by reference to the principles of good public finance which inform its package of domestic tax reforms. The tax and expenditure system of the Community does not accord at all well with sound principles of public finance.

Restraint on the *indirect* taxes which can be levied by a member state will restrict its freedom of action for policy purposes to direct taxation. Simultaneously, the increased mobility of labour will inhibit its freedom of action in the rates of *direct* tax it can levy. Thus, since the public expenditure requirements of member states are not uniform, pressure towards uniformity of several major sources of tax revenue could force some member states into budgetary imbalance or into inappropriate cuts in public expenditure. For example, the pressure to equalise major revenue raising taxes – which the Council accepts as an unavoidable concomitant of integration - could frustrate the pursuit of adjustment or regional policy objectives.

Because of the underdeveloped system of public finance in the Community, pressure for greater uniformity of several major revenue sources in Community countries (in the context of non-uniformity of expenditure requirements) will stop the Community achieving some of its major aims. It will prevent the achievement of a genuine common market and lessen the probability of achieving other Community objectives such as cohesion and convergence - by limiting the pursuit of structural and redistributive policies in member states which require them.

In view of all these considerations, the Council considers that moves towards tax harmonisation should be accompanied by an extension of the fiscal role of the Community. The Council proposes the development of a *permanent system* which facilitates integration, by balancing the moves towards a common tax system with moves towards a shared revenue and expenditure base. This would require the Community to develop a role in certain expenditure programmes - chosen by reference to the most rigorous principles of public finance - in which the Community is not currently involved.

PART IV

Policy Responses

A Strategic approach to European Integration

Ireland has now participated in European integration for sixteen years. The degree of integration already achieved has had a profound impact on the economy and society, and on the autonomy of Irish policy making. We are about to embark on a new phase of European integration which will create substantial threats and opportunities for Irish firms, organisations and citizens, and will reduce further the autonomy of Irish policy in many areas. In the Council's view, the formulation of economic and social policy at the national and Community level, in this rapidly changing environment, must be informed by a conception of what European integration means and what its ultimate objective should be.

The Council has therefore taken the opportunity to stand back and consider the question of European integration. The formulation of a strategic approach to European integration requires the identification of what level of economic integration would be most desirable for Ireland. This must then be combined with knowledge of the *processes* which move, or inhibit movement, of Europe from one stage of integration to another.

THE DESIRABLE LEVEL OF INTEGRATION

In order to identify the desirable level of economic integration we have examined the different types of integrated areas. Although integration is a complex process, which can vary in a large number of ways, three different levels of integration can be defined for the purposes of analysis. *The Customs Union Model* involves only the elimination of tariffs and quotas and adoption of a common external tariff. *The Common Market Model* involves not only free trade but free movement of capital and labour. It also includes some common market-regulating policies, such as competition policy, which in turn implies that a small amount of revenue be raised for a Community budget.

The Economic and Monetary Union Model (EMU) involves

free trade, free movement of capital and labour, plus monetary integration (either a common currency or fixed exchange rates with close co-ordination of the states' macroeconomic policies). In addition, in an EMU many of the policies originally undertaken by the member states will become of concern at the Community level. This requires the existence of a much more substantial Community budget.

We assessed these three levels of economic integration on three criteria: (1) the regional distribution of economic activity and income; (2) microeconomic performance and management; and (3) macroeconomic performance and management. We were particularly interested in how performance under these three headings would affect a small peripheral region in the integrated area.

This investigation led to two conclusions. One concerns the desirable level of integration, and the other concerns what will be required to achieve that level of integration. We now state and explain each of these conclusions.

The first of these is that, on all three criteria, an economic and monetary union emerged as superior for Ireland than either a customs union or a common market. We stress, of course, that by economic and monetary union we mean a Community which has developed sufficient policy competence - that is, sufficient *positive* integration (see panel) - to provide effective macroeconomic management, microeconomic regulation, and balancing redistributive mechanisms.

Positive and Negative Integration

A crucial distinction which has been made throughout the study is that between *negative* and *positive* integration. *Negative* integration refers to the *removal* of tariff or non-tariff barriers to trade or the movement of capital and labour. *Positive* integration consists of the *establishment* of common institutions and policies in order to achieve harmonisation of public policy interventions in the economy, and to achieve other economic and social goals necessary for integration.

1. Arguments for Advanced Economic and Monetary Union

A brief summary of the arguments in favour of economic and monetary union can be given. Under each of the three criteria set out above (regional, microeconomic and macroeconomic) we had to assess the effects of both *market forces* and *public policy*.

The Regional Distribution of Activity and Income

When assessing the regional distribution of activity and income likely to be created by market forces, the Council adopted the view that the effects of *market forces* in shaping the pattern of activity across various regions and member states may not, in fact, be very different at different stages of integration. This conclusion is significant because it questions the more conventional view that the regional costs of integration are confined to, or even arise primarily at, the stage of *monetary* integration.

Indeed, in the Council's view, many of the most important forces making for regional convergence and divergence are inseparable from the internationalisation of economic activity which exists independently of the fact that countries embark on formal integration. Consequently, many of those forces are likely to be influencing Ireland regardless of whether we are in a customs union, a common market, or an economic and monetary union.

In conclusion, our study of the likely regional effects of market forces did not give an emphatic answer to the question: what level of European integration should Ireland favour?

What then of the regional effects of *public policy* in a customs union, a common market, and an economic and monetary union? These are likely to be more favourable in an advanced economic and monetary union, than in lesser stages of integration such as a common market or a customs union. This is because there are strong arguments that successful economic and monetary union requires that the Community tier of government be involved in a wide range of policy functions. While the main argument for this sharing of policy functions between the Community, the national and the local tiers of government, is that it is necessary for genuine economic integration, microeconomic efficiency and macroeconomic management (see below), it does have a regional dimension. This is so because assignment of policy functions, and the associated taxation and expenditure, to the Community tier, will inevitably have some redistributive effects - between persons and between regions – which are likely to be favourable to poorer regions. Indeed existing monetary unions rely heavily on invisible and automatic transfers both between persons and between regions through the central tax system and central social security system, acting as a powerful mitigation of income and activity differentials.

Therefore, taking both *market forces* and *public policy* into account, it seems likely that an adequately structured and rationally organised economic and monetary union is likely to yield a more even distribution of economic activity and income than lesser forms of integration, such as a common market or a customs union.

Microeconomic Performance and Management

One of the central arguments of the NESC report is that the microeconomic benefits of integration are much more likely to be achieved in advanced economic union than in less advanced forms of integration. This is so because the European economies are all mixed economies - that is, economies in which the state plays a significant role. Consider what is involved in creating a genuine common market between *mixed* economies.

First, to achieve a genuinely integrated *market for goods* requires not only the removal of protective tariffs and quotas but also the elimination of borders between states. This, in turn, requires the removal of national technical standards and some harmonisation of indirect tax. It is now clear that these are both very significant steps for national governments to take. But the numerous domestic interventions of a microeconomic kind (such as industrial policy, technology policy, training policy, transport policy, education policy, welfare policy, social policy and health policy) are similar to border interventions *in that they affect competitive conditions* in each country. Therefore, an integrated European market for goods requires some approximate equalisation of this plethora of public influences on competitive conditions in member states. This is clearly very ambitious. Many, but by no means all, of the harmonisation measures required are included in the Community's current 1992 programme.

So far we have only considered what is required for a genuine integration of the market for *goods*. When we consider the creation of an integrated market for labour and capital, further profound implications come to light. The development of a single labour market requires harmonisation of many policies. Fully integrated financial markets would constrain national governments' stabilisation and redistribution policies to such an extent that their realisation seems to be entirely dependent on developments in macroeconomic integration. This puts in perspective what is involved in creating a genuine *common market* and implies that, to all intents and purposes, it requires creation of an *economic and monetary union*.

This means that *the microeconomic benefits of integration are much more likely to be achieved in advanced economic union than in less advanced forms of integration*. This is one of the most important arguments in the NESC's advocacy of advanced economic and monetary union. It is most important that both policy-makers and the public are aware that it is an argument which, if it has validity, has validity for *all* member states. It is not an argument which serves Ireland's interest over and above those of other member states or those of the Community as a whole. It is the Community as a whole, and not Ireland especially, which stands to gain from genuine economic integration, and which stands to sacrifice many of the potential gains if the full implications and requirements of integration are not recognised.

Macroeconomic Performance and Management

There are a number of reasons why the objectives of high growth and low inflation are more likely to be achieved in advanced economic and monetary union than in a common market. Economic and monetary union involves, at the very least, close co-ordination of national macroeconomic policies, while in a common market each country pursues its own macroeconomic policy. But highly interdependent economies will find that that very interdependence thwarts them in their attempts to achieve their macroeconomic goals by means of domestic policy. The classic example of this is the attempt to solve balance of payments deficits by contraction of the domestic economy, which merely passes the problem abroad, and can ultimately lead to little reduction in payments imbalances but a substantial increase in unemployment.

In addition to this general argument in favour of economic and monetary union, there is a specific one which arises because of the changes being introduced in the 1992 programme.

The 1992 programme includes the abolition of controls on the movement of funds between EC countries. This liberalisation of capital markets, in the context of fixed exchange rates, will alter the conditions for the conduct of domestic monetary policy in such a way that it requires either abandonment of fixed exchange rates or greater co-ordination of monetary policy. This proposition is defended with both *theoretical* and *historical* arguments. Analysis shows that to seek to maintain open capital markets, stable exchange rates and autonomous macroeconomic policies is fundamentally inconsistent. The attempt to conduct *independent* macroeconomic policies by a set of countries whose economies are in fact *interdependent* will, in general, impart a deflationary bias to the international system. An historical study of monetary unions and systems strongly supports the proposition that it is not possible to have *at the same time* free trade, freedom from capital restrictions, pegged exchange rates and autonomous macroeconomic policies. If Europe wishes to keep pegged exchange rates it will have to advance to economic and monetary union.

Summary
On all three criteria, regional distribution, microeconomic efficiency and macroeconomic performance, the advanced integration of economic and monetary union seems preferable to lesser forms of integration, such as a customs union or a common market.

Misconceptions about the NESC's Argument
Since publication of the NESC report *Ireland in the European Community* it has been said by a number of commentators that the Council's argument in favour of EMU is based on the hope that the development of the Community budget would involve significant resource transfers to Ireland. Given this supposition, some have argued that this is unrealistic, others that it is undesirable. A look at the arguments spelt out above, or at the detailed arguments of the report itself, should make it clear that these views are somewhat beside the point, because the original premise - that the NESC's argument for EMU is altogether based on the hope of redistribution - is wrong. The Council's argument for advanced integration and the development of Community policies is based on an analysis which shows that such a system is *necessary to achieve genuine integration*. Presentation of the NESC's argument to other Community countries would appeal simultaneously to their rationality and their self interest. It is not, in general, an appeal for their sympathy.

2. Second Conclusion: Political Cohesion

The second important conclusion of our study of different levels of integration is that establishment of substantial Community policies, especially redistributive and macroeconomic policy, requires the creation of a significant degree of 'cohesion' or 'political homogeneity'. Political homogeneity refers to the feeling of belonging to the same political grouping and sharing the same interests and destiny. This has significant implications for a country which perceives its goals as most likely to be achieved in an advanced economic union with a developed Community budget. Its strategic and tactical approach should be oriented to creating that 'degree of cohesion between member states' which would enable functions to be dealt with at the Community level, where there are already strong reasons for doing this. Furthermore, it will not be realistic to see cohesion, as Irish governments seem to have, as *a purely economic* phenomenon which can be achieved prior to, or independently of, 'political homogeneity'. This is because the lack of sufficient 'political homogeneity' or 'degree of cohesion between member states' may then be cited as a reason *not* to allocate a given function to the Community; and yet the formation of a Community policy may be necessary for the achievement of 'cohesion', defined in its narrowly economic sense.

Identification of the desirable level of integration is not sufficient, on its own, for the formulation of Ireland's strategic approach to European integration. Account must also be taken of the *process* by which economic and monetary union might be achieved. Our study of the process of integration has revealed three important findings:

(i) the integration process of a group of democratic states will have a bias towards minimum Community intervention in the economy;

(ii) this tendency is evident in the EC - which is, in fact, developing in an unbalanced manner;

(iii) despite undoubted pressure for further integration it is quite possible that the process of integration can become blocked.

In the Council's view the formulation of a more explicit, coherent and fully articulated European policy or strategy could yield substantial practical benefits to Ireland.

ECONOMIC AND MONETARY UNION AND THE DELORS REPORT

At its meeting in Hanover in June 1988 the European Council established a Committee chaired by Mr Delors, President of the European Commission, to study and propose steps leading towards economic and monetary union. In April 1989 this Committee submitted its report (hereafter referred to as the Delors

Three Fundamental Conclusions of the NESC

There are three fundamental conclusions concerning integration, which informed our consideration of all the detailed policy issues which arise from the impending completion of the internal market.

(1) Economic integration in the narrow sense - the removal of tariff and non-tariff barriers - will not serve to reduce regional disparities and may unleash forces which tend to reinforce existing advantages and disadvantages.

(2) The European Community has developed in an unbalanced manner: the considerable degree of negative integration has not been balanced by sufficient measures of positive integration. This inhibits both the achievement of genuine economic integration and of regional convergence.

(3) Ireland's strategic approach to the European Community should be based on the objective of creating a genuine European economic and monetary union, which would have the characteristics which suit Ireland's social and economic needs and aspirations.

Report) to the European Council.

There is a considerable agreement between general ideas in the Delors Report and the analysis undertaken by the Council. However, on detailed examination, it becomes clear that while the definition of monetary union is similar to that adopted by the Council, the definition of *economic union* is very different. As a result, the vision of economic and monetary union in the Delors Report is quite different from that advocated by the Council.

To understand this statement it is necessary to appreciate the precise nature of the Council's case for economic and monetary union. The Council *defined* EMU as involving not only monetary and macroeconomic policy union, but also Community-level management of a wide range of policies currently undertaken by the member states. The *arguments for* seeking to build *such an* EMU were based on analysis of the likely overall economic performance and the likely regional pattern of income and economic activity. Based on these analyses our conclusion is that both Ireland and the Community as a whole would have a lot to gain from moving to an economic and monetary union of the sort specified in this report. This would ensure that the 1992 programme creates a genuine common market, would secure the monetary stability and macroeconomic progress established in recent years, and would greatly enhance the Community's ability to bring about convergence in living standards.

Overall, the Delors Committee's definition of EMU differs from the NESC's primarily because, though its analytical approach is similar to ours, the Committee has not followed that approach to its logical conclusion and has taken insufficient account of the requirements and implications of genuine economic integration. In particular:

- The Delors Report greatly underestimates the number of policy functions which will have to be shared between the Community and the national tiers of government.
- Although the Delors Report acknowledges that integration can have a negative impact on some regions and insists that monetary union is only conceivable if a high degree of economic convergence is achieved, it does not make allowance for the kind of policy measures which would be necessary to address the regional problem.
- The Report ignores the role which the central budget plays in maintaining macroeconomic balance and achieving economic convergence in existing economic and monetary unions.

Thus, the Delors Report takes insufficient account of the requirements and implications of genuine economic and monetary integration. Ireland should insist that the argument on EMU be widened to include a more adequate analysis of the role of public finance in economic and monetary integration. It should be emphasised that the strong arguments for economic and monetary union apply not only to Ireland but to the Community as a whole. In the Council's view, the entire Community would have much to gain from an economic and monetary union of the type outlined in the report. This would ensure that the 1992 programme creates a genuine common market, would secure the monetary stability and macroeconomic progress established in recent years and would greatly enhance the Community's ability to bring about convergence in living standards.

Dealing with Threats and Opportunities

CORPORATE RESPONSES

It would be both impossible and inappropriate for the NESC to offer a comprehensive or detailed recommendation to businesses on how to prepare for the internal market. Consequently, our discussion of corporate responses should be seen as an identification of some of the main issues which will arise for firms. It also serves to draw out some of the implications of the economic analysis in the rest of the report.

1. Business Strategy

Our analysis of the threats and opportunities shows that the effects of market completion will depend on the specific structure of each industry and on the exact position of firms and products within it. In addition, it should be noted that 1992 is only one of the environmental changes affecting businesses. For some businesses, other factors such as technical change will be far more important than 1992. It follows that no general corporate response can be prescribed in these conclusions. Nevertheless, a number of general points can be made.

One point of great significance has emerged. The terminology of 1992 ('unified internal market', 'single market', 'market of 320 million') has misled many into the belief that most product markets will be genuinely *unified* between now and 1992. However, much of the fragmentation of European markets has little to do with non-tariff barriers, but rather arises from the diversity of cultures, traditions and consumption patterns in Europe. Consequently, many markets will continue to be fragmented after 1992 so that somewhat different products must be designed, created and supplied to each particular market.

The strategic task facing Irish businesses in their planning for 1992 is to identify their particular type of industry and the key determinants of competitive advantage in that industry. Several different ways of categorising markets and defining competitive advantage are referred to in the report. It is frequently the case that particular segments within a given industry may be very different from the industry as a whole and, consequently, the determinants of competitive advantage may be specific to the segment.

The business strategies required of Irish firms are largely strategies for entering foreign markets. The appropriate strategy for achieving this depends upon the nature of the market one is trying to penetrate, the nature of the target country and of the firm itself. Irish firms are generally characterised as late entrants into relatively mature markets. Such markets usually have considerable barriers to entry. There are a variety of strategies available for overcoming or circumventing these barriers, such as co-operative ventures, mergers and acquisitions, sub-supply and technology licencing.

2. Innovation

Process and product innovation have an important role in successful strategies to overcome or circumvent barriers to entry. Pursuit of a strategy of product differentiation through innovation requires, more than anything else, substantial improvements in the *quality of management*. Management is crucial to the correct evaluation of technological options and to the successful pursuit of either product or process innovation.

3. Mergers and Acquisitions

The removal of non-tariff barriers will lead to a restructuring of industries, with mergers and acquisitions becoming increasingly significant. Diversification away from core business is seldom a successful corporate response. A major issue for Irish firms is whether mergers and acquisitions are an appropriate strategy for entering, or making further inroads into, foreign markets. This will depend on the type of industry in question, the degree of concentration, and the extent of market barriers. In highly concentrated industries, for example, in which there are significant entry barriers, acquisitions or joint ventures may be the only feasible way to penetrate foreign markets. In fragmented industries on the other hand, which lack major distribution barriers, it may be possible to build a market position by expansion through direct exports and local distributors.

4. Management Resources

Emphasis on management emerges consistently from our consideration of responses to the threats and opportunities of

1992. It is the task of management to combine all the functional areas of an organisation, to define the segments in which the business can develop and sustain competitive advantage, to devise and implement the strategies which the business will need to compete and to continuously monitor and adapt to a changing environment. Given the existing low level of commitment to management development in Ireland, investment in managerial resources should command priority across all sectors.

5. Financial Services

The findings cited earlier showed that efficiency differences are a greater source of cost differences than size, so the ability of Irish financial institutions to compete on the domestic market against foreign products, and to offer products in foreign markets against local competition, will be crucially influenced by relative efficiency levels between the competing institutions. Exploitation of potential efficiency gains is therefore necessary in the bid to be competitive in the unified internal market.

A second key competitive factor in the financial services market is product innovation. An alternative to in-house product development are joint-venture arrangements – whereby one partner provides the products and the other provides the distribution outlets. Central to the efforts to exploit the scope for efficiency improvements and keep to the forefront in product innovation is the need to adopt the technological advances taking place in telecommunications and data processing. The regulatory changes in the financial services sector expand the options which financial institutions face in penetrating foreign markets. Opportunities for utilising these options are likely in the financially less developed parts of the Community, especially southern Europe. Penetration of foreign markets is likely to take the form of merger/acquisition or various types of alliances. Cracking a foreign market without a significant presence on the ground would prove extremely difficult.

PUBLIC POLICY RESPONSE

1. The Economic Environment

Success in the internal market needs a domestic economic environment conducive to growth and competitive enterprise. This requires continued sound macroeconomic management.

However, creation of the correct economic environment will take on a new meaning in the completed internal market. The increased mobility of goods, labour, and capital will make economic activity more sensitive to taxation and regulation and will, consequently, require significant changes in these areas.

In particular, changes which increase the exposure of the economy to external forces must be complemented by measures which increase the internal efficiency of the Irish economy. This implies, among other things, vigorous implementation of the internal market programme in services such as banking, insurance and transport. Seeking derogations from these measures preserves an uncompetitive domestic structure.

Given the heavily regulated nature of the financial services sector, the actions taken by government are as important as the actions taken by the institutions themselves in preparing to compete in this new environment. Ireland's indigenous institutions must not be handicapped in defending their domestic market, or in launching offensives in new markets, by the domestic taxation and regulatory environment. Two related issues need to be addressed urgently if the indigenous institutions are to position themselves to meet the full rigours of international competition:

(i) the nature of the regulatory structure in an international comparative context;

(ii) the specific taxation of financial institutions and products to ensure fair competition internally and competitive success externally.

The maintenance of an economic environment conducive to growth, and the implementation of other measures in preparation for 1992, requires that the current consensus between the social partners and Government be continued and, indeed, deepened.

2. Industrial Policy

The Council has previously undertaken extensive and detailed work on Ireland's industrial policy. This led the Council to recommend that industrial policy place emphasis on indigenous firms, devise measures to overcome the barriers to entry which face Irish producers, and aim to assist the creation of structurally strong Irish firms. The validity of these recommendations is confirmed when the requirements of completing the internal market are considered.

However, completion of the internal market does require some changes in Ireland's industrial policy:

(i) the scale of firms must become a more important concern of industrial policy;

(ii) policy should aim to increase the ability of firms to *innovate.*

The scale of firms is significant because, in the Council's view, 1992 will bring about further concentration in many industries. In some cases Irish firms will be unable to overcome the advantages which their rivals derive from scale of operation; in such cases these disadvantages must be circumvented or avoided. In other cases, it will be necessary to overcome the difference in scale, and industrial policy should assist this development.

In the Council's view there is a strong case for injecting an innovation orientation into Irish industrial policy. This is necessary because:

- innovation is central to competitive success in many sectors
- firms in peripheral countries and regions tend to undertake less innovation
- the EC is now actively promoting technological development.

3. Competition Policy

It is clear that cross-frontier mergers and take-overs have become much more frequent in recent years and months. In the lead-up to 1992 Irish firms may become increasingly attractive as take-over targets. The question which arises for policy makers is: should they be indifferent as to whether a company is taken over by a domestic or foreign firm?

The Council considers that Ireland cannot be indifferent to foreign take-overs of indigenous business. Each case must be examined on its merits and a decision made on a balance of likely effects. This will require a very close relationship between mergers policy and industrial policy. There is no doubt that some rationalisation of domestic and European competition policy will be required - with the latter becoming involved in issues with a European dimension. However, in the Council's view the Irish dimensions of merger policy must be retained with a strong public interest clause. Under such a public interest clause the investigating authorities would be required to examine the likely external economic effects of any proposed take-over and to balance these against internal effects on the individual businesses, having particular regard to Ireland's industrial policy objectives.

PUBLIC POLICY RESPONSE: AGRICULTURE

In our study of the period since Ireland's accession we identified three problems in the agricultural sector:

(i) The reversal of much of the progress made between 1973 and 1978 and the consequent slow annual average growth of farm incomes in the period since accession;

(ii) The persistence of very low and volatile farm incomes for a sizeable segment of Irish farmers;

(iii) The slow rate of development of the food industry.

The development of farm incomes is related to the domestic inflation rate and the level of agricultural prices. The domestic inflation rate is no longer causing a price-cost squeeze in agriculture. However, the restrictive EC price policy continues and further reform of the CAP is virtually inevitable.

1. Reform of the CAP

In the long run the issue for the Community, and therefore for Ireland as a member of the Community with a great interest in agriculture, is the correct method to adopt to achieve market balance. The Council has previously advocated that greater balance between supply and demand should be achieved by a combination of price and quantitative restrictions, in a context in which support from the Community should be directed more towards solving the low income problems in farming.

Broadly speaking, the Council shares the Community's rejection of the 'free trade' solution advocated by the United States. It favours instead a solution which derives from the Community's traditional approach to market adjustment - that is, an approach which recognises the social dimension of markets and the social costs and benefits which are generated by adjustment to the exigencies of market forces. The Community's rejection of the United States' proposed free trade solution is only tenable on the basis of a new balance between prices and market policies and socio-structural policies.

2. Structural Problems

Solution to the problem of low farm incomes, and of other problems in the agriculture and food industries generally, requires that greater progress be made in solving these structural weaknesses. This in turn requires new approaches at both Community and national level. At Community level the main requirement is further enhancement in the role of socio-structural measures. At domestic level a combination of productivity policy, structural policy and programmes outside agriculture is required.

The formulation of an effective structural policy requires that the objectives of the policy be clarified. They can only be clarified at national level. The Community's rejection of the Mansholt objective of 'economic production units', in favour of maintaining a viable rural population, does *not* resolve the conflict in structural objectives for Ireland. In the Council's view, future Irish structural policy should give priority to achieving *effective land use* rather than to maintaining the maximum number of holdings. But it recommends this structural priority only within the context of complementary productivity policies and non-agricultural programmes.

3. Development of the Food Industry

There is both an industrial and an agricultural dimension to the disappointing progress in the development of Ireland's food processing industry. The agricultural constraints on the development of the food processing industry derive from insecurity, seasonality and non-uniformity of supply of primary agricultural products and from the incentives created by the prevailing prices and markets policy. Overcoming the insecurity, seasonality and non-uniformity of supply requires a strengthening of the structure of Ireland's farm businesses. Given the nature of the market for land this will require a clear and much more vigorous national structural policy.

European Regional Policy

THE STRUCTURAL FUNDS

The Community has three sets of policies aimed at overcoming structural problems which inhibit the economic development of certain regions, enterprises and individuals:

- The European Social Fund (ESF)
- The European Regional Development Fund (ERDF)
- The Guidance Section of the Community agricultural fund.

An important feature shared by these three Structural Funds is their small size relative to the total Community budget, relative to total Community GDP and, most significantly, relative to the scale of inequalities and structural problems in the European economy. The three funds together have increased from 4% of the Community budget in 1972 to over 16% in 1986, and are set to increase to 25% by 1992. However, the EC's budget amounts to only one per cent of Community GDP. Consequently, the Structural Funds account for about a fifth of one per cent of Community GDP. Ireland's share of each of these funds has varied from year to year. Taking the period since accession in 1973 to 1986 as a whole, Ireland's receipts from the three Structural Funds have been dwarfed by receipts in the form of agricultural price supports and subsidies.

EC Grants and Subsidies to Ireland 1973-86	
EAGGF - Guarantee	73.6
EAGGF - Guidance	5.5
ESF	9.6
ERDF	7.1
EMS Interest Subsidies	3.2
Other	0.7
	100.0

For the purpose of EC regional policy the whole of the Republic is treated as a single Community region. This means that central government has had control of funds received from the ERDF, so long as they were spent in line with the criteria set down by the Commission and agreed by the Council of Ministers. Ireland's receipts were spent on a combination of industry/service sector projects and infrastructural investment - with infrastructure absorbing the dominant share.

POLICY ISSUES ARISING FOR IRELAND AND THE COMMUNITY

1. The Role of Community Policy in Creating Convergence

There are four broad types of Community policy which may assist convergence and cohesion.

(i) Structural policies.

(ii) Macroeconomic co-ordination.

(iii) Budgetary or fiscal transfers.

(iv) Differential application of other Community policies, such as agricultural policy or internal market policy.

It is important that both member states and the Community take a broad and realistic view of what can be, and is likely to be, achieved by each of these types of policies in the pursuit of economic and social cohesion.

It seems necessary to conclude that Structural Funds, as currently constituted, will not be sufficient to create convergence, let alone establish equality in regional economic structures and income. It is sometimes argued that the key to regional convergence is the pursuit of sound macroeconomic policies by less developed member states. While sound macroeconomic policies are warranted to avoid inflationary, balance of payments and fiscal problems, there is no validity in the notion that the independent pursuit of low inflation, current account balance and fiscal balance by member states will reduce regional disparities. The limited ability of either structural policies or co-ordinated macroeconomic policy to achieve convergence naturally focuses attention on the possibility of regional redistribution by means of Community taxes and expenditures. Examination of this subject reveals two striking facts. First, there are very strong arguments, in the principles of public finance, for development of the Community budget and re-assignment of policy functions between the tiers of Community government.

Second, in existing economic and monetary unions, normal budgetary contributions and expenditures constitute much the most significant redistributive mechanism between persons, regions and member states. Consequently, there are very strong arguments, on integration, macroeconomic, public finance and equity grounds for considerable and early development of the Community budget. This is one of the central conclusions of our analysis of Ireland's role in the long-term development of the European Community. That analysis shows that the limited scale and ambition of Community policies is likely to frustrate the achievement of its major objectives. Consequently, the extension of Community policy, and the development of the common budget which is the necessary corollary of this, constitutes the major challenge facing European integration. This is why it figures so prominently in the strategic approach to integration advocated by NESC.

Article 130B of the Treaty, introduced by the Single European Act, allows for the differential implementation of Community policies in order to assist economic convergence and cohesion. However, the Council is of the belief that there is a definite but *finite* number of policy areas where it is feasible or advantageous to seek differential application of Community policy under Article 130B.

Conclusion on Policy Approaches to Achieve Convergence

In conclusion, the Council believes that all four policy approaches - structural policy, macroeconomic policy, public finance policy and differential implementation - should be pursued by Ireland. Ireland should be aware, however, that the greatest direct contribution to convergence is likely to arise from the development of the Community budget.

It must also be noted that if Ireland is to argue that regional convergence is a shared Community objective and responsibility, and to advocate that Community policies to achieve it be adopted on a realistic scale, then Ireland itself must be capable of making a leading contribution to the formulation of those policies. Both the objective and the policies to achieve it must be advocated by argument of the highest quality.

2. The Content of Regional Policy

The *content* of regional policy is at least as important as the amount of money spent. It is important that structural policy measures, funded jointly by the Community and the national government, should be aimed at removing the constraints on the development of the Irish economy, rather than being designed in response to the eligibility criteria set down by the Commission. Our first conclusion on the *content* of structural policy in the current context is that it should involve a *balance* between investments in *industrial* and rural development policy and investments in *infrastructure*. Industrial policy should now involve the following elements:

- concentration on indigenous firms
- an attempt to increase the innovation potential of Irish firms
- a focus on the scale of Irish firms where this is appropriate.

In choosing infrastructure projects the following should be taken into consideration:

- It is important that infrastructure not be equated with transport infrastructure. Telecommunications, water, drainage and other environmental structures can be at least as important.
- In general, the strongest economic arguments for road improvement are based on the needs of passenger traffic rather than freight.
- Improved access to the European market may require changes in regulation and taxation instead of, or as well as, new infrastructural investments.
- Improvement of transport infrastructure pursued in isolation could do more harm than good. It is vital that, simultaneously with the improvement in access to foreign markets, the *ability* of domestic firms, and individuals, *to respond* to market opportunities is enhanced by industrial and other policies.

The Social Dimension

The social dimension of the integrated European market is essentially a continuation of the EC's social policy in two respects. First, the context of the social dimension reflects the traditional mix of research, pilot and experimental interventions and promotion of general social objectives. Secondly, the social dimension is relatively small scale in terms of resources and activities. However, a new ingredient in EC social policy is observable - a recognition that the full development of the Community and the completion of the market will require more coherent and substantial policies. This recognition has yet to be developed and translated into agreed policies and programmes.

A strong and necessary interplay between the 'social' and the 'market' dimensions is stressed by the Commission. The Commission deems it *necessary,* to incorporate social elements into the market completion programme. This necessity derives, in the Commission's analysis, from the logic of integration. For example, integration will require freer movement of labour and, therefore, more harmonised social security and other provisions; the more uniform cost environment required for free competition will impose less diversity in the social/regulatory framework. In the Commission's analysis, therefore, the analytic connection between the process of integration and its social framework and consequences is undeniable and strong. This perspective on the social dimension, which sees it as a necessary extension of the internal market, is consistent with the analysis of integration which informs the entire report of the NESC.

The Council considers that inter-personal redistribution, currently effected through member states' social security, health and education systems, should now be considered in the light of the public finance principles appropriate to an integrated economy. On this basis there may be grounds for part Community financing of domestic programmes. In particular, at this point in the evolution of the Community, as a unified labour market emerges, there are grounds for communal sharing of the costs of unemployment compensation. Clearly, the Council is not advocating immediate and complete centralisation of social policy programmes. The essential point is that the principles of public finance dictate the levels in the Community at which activities and services are funded. Such principles would suggest that there are now grounds for partial centralisation of specific programmes. This point is of particular relevance to the social dimension as it is in the area of social and labour market provisions that these questions most directly arise.

15

Concluding Remarks

Completion of the internal market will result in the Irish economy becoming more integrated into the European economy. Inefficiency will now be penalised as never before. With the increase in mobility of goods, labour, investment and financial capital, all national policies and activities must be considered in a new light. Changes which increase the exposure of the economy to external forces must be complemented by measures which enhance the internal efficiency of the Irish economy. This requires changes by all elements of our society.

The Council is absolutely clear that Ireland's future lies in the fullest participation in the European Community. The central argument in this report is that full economic, monetary and social integration is in Ireland's best interest. However, the Council is well aware of the problems and difficulties that have been, and will be, experienced in the process of integration. Indeed this report provides detailed empirical and theoretical analysis of these problems. Having considered the benefits of advanced integration, and the difficulties which can arise at various stages of integration, the Council has concluded that there are two prime requirements for Ireland:

(i) a clear national strategy for European integration which will provide a guide to external negotiations and domestic decision-making;

(ii) continued consensus among the social partners, at the national level, and at the level of the firm, to ensure a swift and flexible response that is most conducive to the objectives of fuller employment, higher living standards and a better social framework.

The Council is confident that if these requirements are met, Ireland should be well placed to take full advantage of the opportunities inherent in the current phase of European integration. Otherwise, there is a strong likelihood that Ireland's performance over the next decade will show little improvement over that of the 1972-86 era.

NATIONAL ECONOMIC AND SOCIAL COUNCIL

Constitution and Terms of Reference

1. The main task of the National Economic and Social Council shall be to provide a forum for discussion of the principles relating to the efficient development of the national economy and the achievement of social justice, and to advise the Government, through the Taoiseach, on their application. The Council shall have regard, inter alia, to:

(i) the realisation of the highest possible levels of employment at adequate reward,

(ii) the attainment of the highest sustainable rate of economic growth,

(iii) the fair and equitable distribution of the income and wealth of the nation,

(iv) reasonable price stability and long-term equilibrium in the balance of payments,

(v) the balanced development of all regions in the country, and

(vi) the social implications of economic growth, including the need to protect the environment.

2. The Council may consider such matters either on its own initiative or at the request of the Government.

3. Members of the Government will meet regularly with NESC on their initiative or on the initiative of NESC to discuss any matters arising from the terms of reference and in particular to discuss specific economic and social policy measures and plans and to explore together proposals and actions to improve economic and social conditions. Any reports which the Council may produce shall be submitted to the Government, and shall be laid before each House of the Oireachtas and published.

4. The membership of the Council shall comprise a Chairman appointed by the Government in consultation with the interests represented on the Council, and

Five persons nominated by agricultural organisations,

Five persons nominated by the Confederation of Irish Industry, Federation of Irish Employers and the Construction Industry Federation,

Five persons nominated by the Irish Congress of Trade Unions,

Six other persons appointed by the Government, including one from the National Youth Council of Ireland,

The Secretary of the Departments of Finance, Industry and Commerce and Labour.

Any other Government Department shall have the right of audience at Council meetings if warranted by the Council's agenda, subject to the right of the Chairman to regulate the numbers attending.

5. The term of office of members shall be for five years. Casual vacancies shall be filled by the Government or by the nominating body as appropriate. Members filling casual vacancies may hold office until the expiry of the other members' current term of office.

6. The numbers, remuneration and conditions of service of staff are subject to the approval of the Taoiseach.

7. The Council shall regulate its own procedure.

NATIONAL ECONOMIC AND SOCIAL COUNCIL MEMBERS*

Chairman: Mr. Pádraig Ó hUiginn

Nominated by the Government

Mr. John Curry
Dr. Miriam Hederman O'Brien
Ms. Sylvia Meehan
Mr. Kevin Murphy
Dr. Fergus O'Ferrall
Mr. Michael Webb
Mr. Seán Cromien

Nominated by the Confederation of Irish Industry

Mr. Leo O'Donnell
Mr. Liam Connellan

Nominated by the Irish Congress of Trade Unions

Mr. Philip Flynn
Mr. Dan Murphy
Mr. Peter Cassells
Mr. Kieran Mulvey
Ms. Patricia O'Donovan

Nominated by the Irish Co-operative Organisation Society

Mr. Gregory Tierney

Nominated by the Irish Creamery Milk Suppliers' Association

Mr. Donal Hynes
Mr. Ciaran Dolan

Nominated by the Irish Employers Confederation

Mr. Thomas Toner
Mr. John Dunne
Mr. David Kennedy

Nominated by the Irish Farmers' Association

Mr. Thomas Clinton
Mr. Michael Berkery

**During the course of this study the following also served on the Council:*

Dr. Eugene McCarthy, Federated Union of Employers
Mr. David Medcalf, National Youth Council of Ireland
Mr. Donal Nevin, Irish Congress of Trade Unions.